In the Street

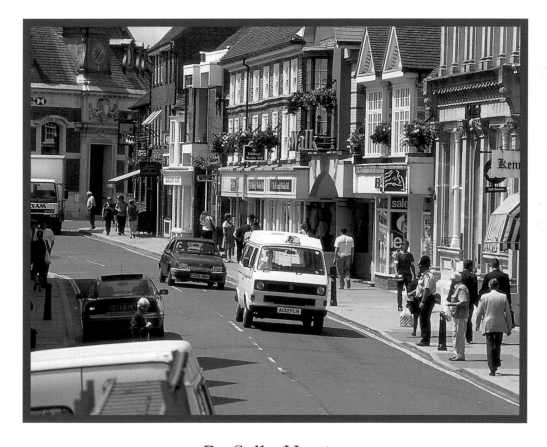

By Sally Hewitt
Photographs by Chris Fairclough

FRANKLIN WATTS
LONDON • SYDNEY

This edition 2003

Franklin Watts
96 Leonard Street
London EC2A 4XD

Franklin Watts Australia
45-51 Huntley Street
Alexandria
NSW 2015

Editor: Samantha Armstrong
Designer: Louise Snowdon
Consultant: Steve Watts, School of Education, University of Sunderland

A CIP catalogue record for this book is
available from the British Library
Dewey Decimal Classification Number: 388.4

ISBN 0 7496 5200 4

Printed in Malaysia

Contents

What is a street?

Some streets are busy with people and cars. The street in the picture below has shops on both sides of it.

• How do you know if cars are allowed in this street?

In this picture, there is not much traffic and hardly any people. This is a country lane.

• What do you think makes a street?

Your street

People live in the houses that line both sides of this street. There are gates, hedges and walls outside the houses.

- What kind of street do you live in?
- Do you think you would like to live here?

• Why do you think cars are parked half on the
pavement and half on the road?
• What does it mean for people using the pavement?

When the pavement is blocked by cars or
wheelie bins it is difficult for people to get past.

Think about your street and how it is different,
or the same, as this one.

Village street

This street only has a few shops.
There are also houses on it.

• What do you think the shops sell?

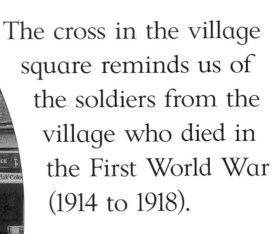

The cross in the village square reminds us of the soldiers from the village who died in the First World War (1914 to 1918).

• Do you think the buildings behind the cross were meant to be shops when they were first built?

The blue sign points to a special event in the village.

• Look at the main picture to see where the visitors will park their cars and coaches.

City street

This street is in a city.

- What different ways of travelling about can you see?
- What sounds would you hear on this street?
- Do you think it would be quiet or noisy?

Pedestrians are people who are walking, not driving or riding a bicycle.

- What can you see in the street that helps to keep pedestrians safe?
- What is the white and yellow bollard in the middle of the street for?

Look closely at the photograph.

- There are lots of shops in the street. Can you find any of these shops in a street near you?
- When shops close, the doors are locked. How do you think the news stand at the bottom of the picture closes at night?

No cars allowed

A street where no cars are allowed is called a precinct.

• Think about the differences between a precinct and an ordinary street.

Bollards stop traffic
driving in the precinct.

- How do you think
goods are delivered
to the shops here?
- What are the people doing
that they wouldn't be able to
do in an ordinary street?

There are bins for people
to put their litter in.

- What else can you see in
the main picture that is useful
for pedestrians?

- Why do you think
these bicycles have
been locked to
the cycle stands?

15

Shopping street

On a busy shopping street people and traffic come and go all day. A policeman in uniform is on duty.

- What do you think the different people in the street are doing?

There is a bank at the end of the street.

- What other kinds of buildings can you see?

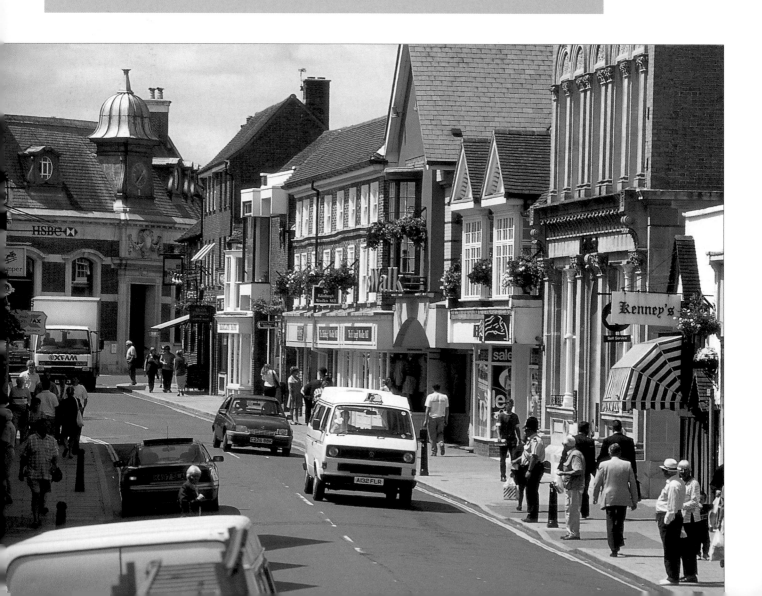

Some streets have lots of different types of shops.

- What makes you want to go inside this shop?

People work inside and outside the shops.

- Why is it important for shops to have clean windows?
- What difference do they make to the street?

- Who do you think looks after these hanging baskets?

Crossing the street

A pedestrian crossing is the safest place for people to cross the street. The traffic stops to allow people across safely to the other side.

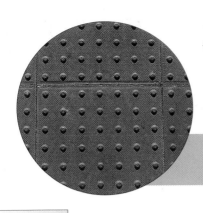

At the crossing you can feel these bumps in the pavement when you walk over them.

• Why do you think the bumps are there?

Press the button and the traffic lights will change.

• How do you know if the button has been pressed?

When the green man lights up, people can cross the street safely.

• What can the people hear as they use the crossing?

Slow down!

There are a lot of cars on this street. Look closely at the picture to see what other vehicles might use the street too.

- Can you see to the end of this very long, straight street?

There is a bus stop on both sides of the street.

• How far do you have to walk from your house to a bus stop?

Give way to oncoming vehicles

This is the other side of the sign in the main picture. It tells the traffic to stop to allow the cars coming towards them through. When the street is clear, they can go.

• Why do you think the cars have to slow down or stop here?

One-way street

Traffic is only allowed to drive one way down this street.

• What do you notice about the way the cars are parked?

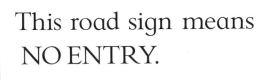

This road sign means
NO ENTRY.

• Who is the sign meant for?

The white triangle on the road
tells drivers to get ready to stop.

• Why do you think traffic
has to stop here?
• What other road markings
can you see?

Cleaning up

A street sweeper has an important job to do.
Wet leaves make the street slippery.
Rubbish and leaves in the gutters block the drains
so the street floods when it rains.

The street sweeper has this sign on the back.

- What does it mean?

The sweeper's brush is on an arm that moves the brush into different positions. It whirls around very fast.

- When do you think the brush needs to be lifted off the ground?

Look how clean the street is where the sweeper has been.

- How can you help to keep the streets clean?

Night street

It's night time. All kinds of different
lights light up this street.
Street lamps shine down on the pavement.
The driver of the car has it's lights on.
It is important to see and be seen if you
are travelling about in the dark.

•How would a cyclist make sure they
could be seen?
•Why do you think the shops have lights on
when they are closed?
•What other kinds of lights can you see?

Key words

Bollard
a post to stop traffic entering the area.

Drain
where rainwater pours underneath the street. Drains help to keep streets dry.

Driver
a driver is the person who sits at the steering wheel of a car, lorry or bus and drives it along.

Gutter
the gutter is a channel at the edge of the street for collecting rainwater.

Pavement
the pavement is the part of the street where pedestrians walk. Traffic is not allowed on the pavement.

Pedestrian crossing
where traffic stops for pedestrians to cross the street.

Pedestrians
people who are walking along, not driving or riding a bike.

Precinct
a street for pedestrians only. No traffic is allowed.

Shop
a place where things are bought and sold.

Sign
a sign tells you things you need to know. It may point the way or give you a warning.

Street
a road with houses, shops or buildings on either side.

Traffic
the name for cars, lorries, buses or bikes.

Get to know your street

1. Make a chart showing different types of street.
   Ask the children in your class what type of street
   they live on.
   - Is it busy or quiet?
   - Is it a one-way street?
   - Does everyone live in a street?

2. Draw a map of the streets you go along to get to school.

3. Find out what is in your street.
   - How many houses are there?
   - How many lamp posts are there?
   - Are there any shops?

4. Make a note of everything in the street your school
   is on that helps to make it safe.

5. Draw a picture of a street where you would like
   to live.
   - Is it like your street?
   - How is it different?

Index